MW00977722

Swimming

Swimming

THOMAS JAGER

Five-time Olympic Medal Swimmer
Founder of the Gold Medal Swimming Clinics, Inc.
Tijeras, New Mexico

Series Editor
SCOTT O. ROBERTS, Ph.D.

Department of Health, Physical Education, and Recreation
Texas Tech University
Lubbock, Texas

Boston   Burr Ridge, IL   Dubuque, IA   Madison, WI
New York   San Francisco   St. Louis
Bangkok   Bogotá   Caracas   Lisbon   London   Madrid   Mexico City
Milan   New Delhi   Seoul   Singapore   Sydney   Taipei   Toronto

WCB/McGraw-Hill

A Division of The **McGraw-Hill** Companies

WINNING EDGE SERIES: SWIMMING

◎ This book is printed on recycled, acid-free paper containing 10% postconsumer waste.

2 3 4 5 6 7 8 9 0 DOC/DOC 9 3 2

ISBN 0–8151–4853–4

Publisher: *Edward E. Bartell*
Executive editor: *Vicki Malinee*
Editorial coordinator: *Tricia R. Musel*
Senior marketing manager: *Pamela S. Cooper*
Project manager: *Brenda K. Lahey-Paisley*
Production supervisor: *Deborah Donner*
Coordinator of freelance design: *Michelle D. Whitaker*
Senior photo research coordinator: *Lori Hancock*
Supplement coordinator: *David A. Welsh*
Compositor: *Shepard Poorman Communications Corp.*
Typeface: *10/12 Palatino*
Printer: *R.R. Donnelley & Sons Company/Crawfordsville, IN*

Cover image: © *Bill Leslie Photography*

1520-9849

www.mhhe.com

PREFACE

Swimming is a growing sport for people of all ages and various abilities. It is truly a participation sport; hence, no one sits on the bench. Whether you swim during the summer at a public pool or swim all-year-round at the local YMCA, swimming is a sport that lasts a lifetime. The health benefits of swimming are unequaled when compared to other sports. *Swimming* is designed to teach you effective stroke techniques and workout drills to improve your swimming. Swimmers must be students of the sport if they are to learn the challenging and calming sport of swimming.

▶ Audience

This text is designed for anyone who loves swimming as well as students in academic courses on swimming. The book is intended to be an easy-to-read, useful tool that provides information about how to develop and improve your swimming.

▶ Features

The information in this text can be used at any level of swimming because it contains basic rules and guidelines. The introductory chapters provide an overview of the history of the sport, selecting equipment, the fitness aspect of swimming, and the basic skills and terminology.

As an Olympic Gold Medal swimmer, Jager knows the most intricate details of each stroke. He writes about beginning strokes such as the sidestroke and the elementary stroke and goes on to cover freestyle, backstroke, breaststroke, and the butterfly.

You will find professional photographs of Jager and other swimmers demonstrating proper form and technique in the water. The illustrations of proper form and technique are an excellent tool for self-evaluation and a guide for improvement.

In addition, this text offers special features that enhance its use:

- Each chapter has a bulleted list of objectives and a closing summary to reinforce the major points covered.
- Key terms are highlighted in boldface type and are also defined. This feature enables you to build a working vocabulary of concepts and principles necessary for beginning, developing, and improving your swimming.
- Performance Tip boxes outlines safety-minded concepts, drills, applications, and procedures. These provide a quick review of important information and help to enhance results.

- One of the chapters includes the workout examples for all different skill levels (i.e., beginning, intermediate, advanced). The schedules allow you to utilize the workout assessments to improve your fitness.

▶ Ancillaries

To facilitate use of this text in the classroom, a printed Test Bank is available to instructors. These questions, ranging from true/false to short-answer formats, allow for quick assessment of the basic concepts of swimming.

▶ Acknowledgments

I would like to thank the following reviewers who provided me with expert commentary during the development of this text: Amanda Alms, Ray Riordon, Jan Hardcastle, John McVan, and instructors from California University at Long Beach, Stanford University, and Marshall University.

I would also like to extend a special thanks to my parents Bob and Harriet Jager for driving me to workout every day for over a decade. To my coaches—Penny Taylor, the retired founder of Parkway Swim Club, and Ron Ballatore at UCLA during the 80s and the 90s—who are two essential and important people responsible for my swimming career. And a final thanks goes to my wife Becky for her unconditional support to the sport of swimming.
—Tom Jager

CONTENTS

CHAPTER 1

A BRIEF HISTORY OF SWIMMING

Objectives

After reading this chapter, you should be able to do the following:

- Discuss what swimming is all about.
- Give a basic history of the sport of swimming.
- Name some well-known swimmers.

KEY TERMS

While reading this chapter, you will become familiar with the following terms:

- ► Easter Island Swimming Race
- ► Duke Paoa Kahanamoku
- ► Esther Williams
- ► Johnny Weissmuller
- ► Mark Spitz

Swimming, like sports in general, is affected by current trends in society. Today, swimming is enjoying a rebirth as a healthy choice for exercise. More doctors are sending patients to the pool for physical therapy and conditioning. The reason is very simple—anyone, at any age, can learn to swim or exercise in the water. There is no jolting or pounding on joints and tendons. This sport exercises the heart, the muscles, and the mind, without straining the body.

Until 1956, there were only three recognized swimming strokes—the freestyle, the backstroke, and the breaststroke. A fourth stroke, the butterfly, which was developed in the 1930s, was recognized as a separate stroke in the 1950s.

Swimming is a dynamic sport that challenges both mind and body. You can participate in the sport as an individual or as part of a team. It can be done competitively, for fitness, or simply for recreation. Swimming could save your life or someone else's. And when you get to the point where you can swim with ease, peace of mind will follow.

A HISTORICAL PERSPECTIVE

Since the first strokes were taken, there have been swimming competitions. One race that has survived history occurred on **Easter Island** in the South Pacific. The local people participated in a grueling duathlon: hike, swim, hike. The race determined who would be king of the island for one year. The race began on the edge of a volcano. Participants would swim to a small island to the west, find a specific sea bird egg, swim back, and place the unbroken egg in the same place the race began. The swimmers transported their eggs by wrapping them in bandannas and swimming across the ocean with the eggs tied to their foreheads, which is a similar position used in freestyle today. That is, keeping the head still and straight forward on the surface of the water. This Easter Island Race demanded the same elements as modern day swimming competition—preparation and efficiency in the water.

The beginning of the twentieth century produced many of swimming's most notable modern-day competitors, not only for their roles as swimmers, but also for their roles as actors. **Duke Paoa Kahanamoku**, a native Hawaiian, along with other native Hawaiians, dominated the U.S. Olympic team in the early 1900s. The Duke was the most famous and charismatic of the team. He transformed freestyle into what is now considered the classical freestyle form and won two gold medals for his efforts. He also was a key figure in the development and popularity of surfing. He acted in over thirty movies and became the official greeter of Hawaii.

Esther Williams swam her way into people's hearts by showing them a more elegant aspect of water sports by performing water ballet, also known as synchronized swimming. For 20 years, in both movies and television, Buster Crabbe and **Johnny Weissmuller** played the role of competent swimmer, Tarzan. Eleanor Holm, a gold medalist in the 100-meter backstroke in the 1932 Olympic games, starred in *Tarzan's Revenge* (1936).

Swimming became popular again in the 1970s due to the successes of the United States Olympic swim teams. The most notable star, **Mark Spitz**, made history by winning seven gold medals in the 1972 summer Olympics in Munich.

SUMMARY

- Swimming is a great sport for exercising; it's easy on the muscles and tendons.
- Since the first strokes were taken, swimmers have engaged in competitive races such as the Easter Island Race.

- Well-known swimmers like Duke Paoa Kahanamoku, Esther Williams, Johnny Weissmuller, and Mark Spitz each contributed significant milestones to the sport of swimming.

▶ **Easter Island Swimming Race**

A competitive swimming race that occurred on Easter Island in the South Pacific.

▶ **Duke Paoa Kahanamoku**

A swimmer and actor who transformed the freestyle and won two gold medals in the Olympics.

▶ **Esther Williams**

Known for her elegant qualities in the water sport of synchronized swimming.

▶ **Johnny Weissmuller**

Played the role of competent swimmer, Tarzan, in both television and film.

▶ **Mark Spitz**

A swimmer who made history by winning seven gold medals in the 1972 summer Olympics in Munich.

THE **FITNESS** ASPECT

Objectives

After reading this chapter, you should be able to do the following:

- List the basic rules of water safety.
- Discuss the lifelong benefits of swimming.
- Identify the two main national organizations involved in competitive swimming.

KEY TERMS

While reading this chapter, you will become familiar with the following terms:

- ► Water Safety
- ► Lifeguards
- ► Panic

- ► Fitness Swimming
- ► United States Swimming (USS)

WATER SAFETY

The most basic function of learning to swim is to become safe and confident around water. **Water safety** skills benefit you and those around you. A lack of swimming knowledge can put you at risk. Before entering any pool there are a few basic rules every swimmer should know.

NO UNSUPERVISED SWIMMING

No one should ever swim alone or without proper supervision. A certified lifeguard watching the pool is the best safeguard. **Lifeguards** serve a valuable function around pools—saving lives and maintaining order. The American Red Cross certifies lifeguards throughout the United States.

FIGURE 2-1 Pool markings indicating no diving.

FIGURE 2-2 Enter the pool feet first.

▶ **Water Safety**
All swimmers need to understand and practice water safety techniques in order to protect themselves and others from serious, even fatal, injuries.

▶ **Lifeguards**
The American Red Cross certifies lifeguards across the country. A lifeguard is a skilled swimmer who is trained to manage emergency situations.

Safety Tips

- Locate lifeguard.
  A lifeguard should be present on the pool deck before entering the water.
- Check clarity of water.
  The swimmer should be able to see the bottom of the pool.
- Check depth of water.
  Entering shallow water can be dangerous. Enter feet first and slowly.
- Evaluate swimmer's physical condition.
  Is the swimmer too tired, too cold, or too inebriated to swim?

NO DIVING

Head injuries, unfortunately, are common swimming accidents. The majority of accidents occur in water less than 5 feet deep by swimmers who have not properly investigated the water conditions. Swimmers should always check the clarity and depth of the water before entering the pool. The safest way to enter the water is feet first. A competitive swimmer or diver should be taught by a professional instructor about *where* and *how* to dive into a pool.

NO RUNNING

The pool deck, the area immediately surrounding the pool, will most likely be wet and slippery. The pool deck can be just as hazardous as the water. Running and horseplay around the pool can lead to unnecessary injuries.

DO NOT PANIC

Panic is sudden and overpowering terror. Panic during a swimming accident can lead to more serious problems. It is important to maintain a calm presence during any accident situation. Panic can overwhelm even the best swimmer. The more you learn about the water and water safety, the more confidence you will have around the water, which will lower the risk of panic.

NO ALCOHOL OR DRUGS

Maintain mental and physical control at all times around the pool or any body of water.

FITNESS SWIMMING

The fitness swimmer swims for exercise. The benefits of **fitness swimming** as a form of exercise are clear. Swimming is a low-impact exercise. The water is a gentle medium and there is very little stress to the tendons, joints, or bones. The body floats while the heart, lungs, and muscles work. The sport of swimming is a lifetime sport. Anyone can learn to swim, at any age.

GOOD FOR THE MIND

Swimming is a solitary sport that can offer hours of uninterrupted privacy while exercising. When your face is in the water, there is no discussion or outside distraction hindering your concentration. As your swimming improves, less energy is spent trying to stay afloat; allowing more energy to be spent on contemplation. This solitude may be the most rewarding health benefit—and the most overlooked. The rhythmic breathing and increased oxygen intake, combined with exercising and stretching the body, help relax the swimmer. Fitness swimming is quickly becoming the sport of choice for many people looking for stress relief. When the swimmer puts on goggles and starts to swim, the rest of the world is easily left behind.

GOOD FOR TENDONS AND LIGAMENTS

The body's buoyancy in the water eases pressure and stress to all joints in the body. While swimming you are able to work the heart without injuring the body. Swimming will help with the body's overall flexibility, which leads to good all-around health and well being.

GOOD FOR THE HEART

Swimming is good for your heart and will help you get into great shape. At what rate and to what result ultimately depends on the individual swimmer. Any exercise will increase your heart rate, force you to take in more oxygen, and create greater blood flow. The more you exercise those basic body functions, the better you will feel. There are two ways to measure and manipulate your swimming program in order to find out if you are getting in shape. One way is to simply count

▶ **Panic**
A sudden and overwhelming feeling of terror.

▶ **Fitness Swimming**
Swimming is an excellent sport for exercise because it is easy on your tendons and joints as well as a great muscle workout.

the number of lengths you swim during a prescribed amount of time. Find a comfortable pace to swim ("a walking pace"). Time yourself for 20 minutes and count the number of lengths swum. If you swim consistently, over time you will find the number of lengths you can swim at a comfortable pace. In the prescribed 20 minutes you will increase the number of lengths.

The second way to increase the cardiovascular output in a swimming program is to increase the intensity of the workout. Changing speed during a swim workout will help increase heart rate. There are many different types of swimming exercise and training methods to increase your intensity during training. See chapter 10, Workout Schedules: Vital to Fitness, for further information.

Above all, a consistent commitment to a swimming program will offer the best physical results. In order to give any new exercise a true effort, a minimum of 3 to 6 months of consistent practicing, two to three times a week should be planned from the beginning.

SWIMMING AND WEIGHT LOSS

Swimming is not the fastest way to lose weight, but it is one of the safest. The pressures and stress of jogging and other exercises are compounded by added weight.

TOTAL BODY EXERCISE

Swimming does not isolate one particular muscle group or muscle. Swimming uses upper body, lower body, chest, and back muscles equally.

CONTROLLED BREATHING EXERCISE

One way to focus attention on the body and relieve stress is to concentrate using a controlled breathing pattern. Swimming forces the swimmer into a breathing pattern, no matter what stroke you are swimming or how fast. Many swimmers come to the pool to break away from the daily grind. A controlled breathing exercise is a age-old method of obtaining some peace of mind.

The factors above translate into a great sport any person can participate in, at any age!

COMPETITIVE SWIMMING

The competitive swimmer swims for exercise and competition. There are many opportunities to compete in the sport of swimming. Two national organizations offer local swimming programs for every level and ability for the competitive swimmer, both young and old. **United States Swimming** Inc. (USS) is the national

FIGURE 2-3 A swim meet in progress.

governing body for competitive swimming. United States Masters Swimming (USMS) is the national organization that organizes competitions for athletes over the age of 19 years. Local YMCAs have programs for the age group swimmers and masters swimmer. Many high schools, colleges, and universities across the country also offer competitive swim programs. And finally, our local community centers and neighborhood associations may have summer programs available.

SUMMARY

- Water safety skills benefit everyone. Remember the following rules when around a pool: no swimming without a lifeguard, investigate water conditions before diving, no running on pool deck, never panic when you are in the water, and maintain mental and physical control while in the water.
- Swimming is an excellent way to gain better personal fitness because it uses all muscles.
- The United States Swimming Inc. (USS) and the United States Masters Swimming (USMS) are two national organizations people may get involved in if they are interested in competitive swimming.

▶ **United States Swimming (USS)**
   United States Swimming is the governing body for age group swimming in the United States.

CHAPTER 3

FACILITIES AND EQUIPMENT FOR THE SPORT

Objectives

After reading this chapter, you should be able to do the following:

- Illustrate the dimensions and setup of a swimming pool.
- Describe the basic equipment.
- Take proper care of the equipment.

KEY TERMS

While reading this chapter, you will become familiar with the following terms:

► Short Course Pool   ► Cap

► Long Course Pool   ► Kick Board

► Lane Lines   ► Pull-buoy

► Starting Blocks   ► Training Paddles

► Goggles

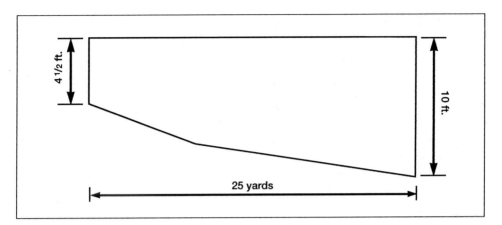

FIGURE 3-1 25-yard pool (U.S. standard length pool).

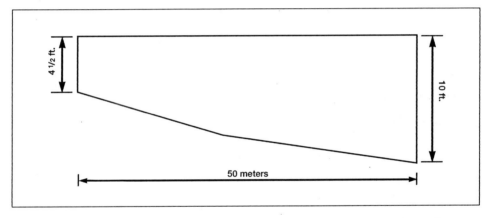

FIGURE 3-2 50-meter pool (Olympic and world standard length pool).

Swimming pools come in all shapes and sizes. Pools can be indoors or outdoors, public or private, and small or large. Pools are found at YMCAs, health clubs, tennis clubs, boy's and girl's clubs, public parks, and in backyards all over the world.

POOL DIMENSIONS AND SETUP

A 25-yard pool is the most common in the United States, and is commonly referred to as a **short course pool**. A **long course pool** is 50 meters in length and is

▶ **Short Course Pool**
  A short course pool is 25 yards long.

▶ **Long Course Pool**
  A long course pool is 50 meters long.

used for Olympic and international competitions. These pools can have four, six, or eight lanes. Most modern pools are at least 4 1/2 feet deep at one end and can gradually descend to 16 feet deep at the other end.

LANE LINES

Lane lines are plastic buoys strung together on a line dividing the pool into lanes. They keep the swimmers from swimming into each other and help to decrease water turbulence—waves created by a swimmer moving through the water.

FIGURE 3-3 Lane lines divide the pool into separate lanes.

PACE CLOCK

Most pools are equipped with a pace clock. It is an oversized clock that is visible from the water. It is used for interval training or timing your swim.

FIGURE 3-4 Pace clock.

BACKSTROKE FLAGS

Backstroke flags are positioned at least 5 feet above the water's surface and 5 yards from each end of the pool (or 5 meters in a long course pool). These flags are commonly called "backstroke flags," because they give the backstroker a visual warning that he or she is approaching the wall.

STARTING BLOCKS

Starting blocks are platforms mounted at the deep end of a pool upon which the swimmers stand at the start of competitive races. The starting block can be no more than 27 inches above the water's surface. For safety reasons, blocks should be

FIGURE 3-5 Backstroke flags and starting blocks found in a competition.

placed at the deep end of the pool or over water that is at least 4 1/2 feet deep. The top of the starting block should have a nonslip surface.

EQUIPMENT

Like all sports, some swimmers buy expensive equipment, while others get by with just a suit and goggles.

Equipment Tip

Chlorine can damage all swimming equipment. Rinsing equipment after every use will prolong the life of your swimming gear.

▶ **Lane Lines**
Lane lines divide the pool into separate lanes and help reduce water turbulence.

▶ **Starting Blocks**
Starting blocks are the platforms upon which competitive swimmers stand when starting a race.

THE SUIT

There are two types of materials used for swimsuits today: nylon and lycra. A nylon suit is the preferred choice for fitness swimming because the material resists chlorine and lasts longer. A nylon suit is often hard to find and offers less comfort than a lycra suit. Most stores carry lycra suits, which are more versatile, satisfying all swimming activities. Many swimmers wear lycra suits for workout and competition. The fabric does not hold water and gives with the movement of the body, while offering a tight fit. The lycra suit is considered a lighter and faster swimsuit.

Chlorine will cause all swimsuits to wear out rapidly. Therefore, it is best to rinse your swimsuit and all equipment after every use.

THE GOGGLES

The **goggles** are the second most important piece of equipment. Goggles enable you to see better and protect your eyes from the chlorine. Goggles come in many shapes and sizes. It is important to find a pair that fits your face comfortably. There is nothing mare frustrating than wearing a pair of goggles that leak or gouge your nose. Leaks are not always caused by a loose strap or nosepiece; the goggle design may not fit your face. Try on several different styles before making your selection. Fit is the most important consideration.

THE CAP

The swim **cap** rounds out the basic equipment. Swimmers wear swim caps to keep their hair covered and protected from the chlorine. However, they do not last long. There are two types of material used today: latex and silicon. The latex cap is the most popular choice because it is lighter and more flexible compared to the heavier silicon cap. The best way to maintain the cap is to rise the chlorine off and dry the cap before putting it into your swim bag.

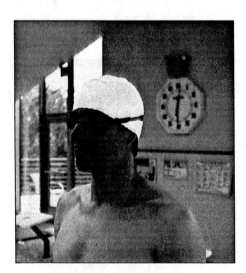

FIGURE 3-6 Cap and goggles.

ADDITIONAL EQUIPMENT

There are many training aids, none of which are necessary to train or enjoy swimming. However, they can be used to increase the effectiveness of your stroke or kick.

The **kick board** is the most-used training tool in swimming. The kick board isolates the kick, which increases the leg workout. To use prop-

FIGURE 3-7 Additional equipment: paddle, pull-buoy, kick board, cap and goggles, and fins.

erly, hold the board out in front of you and grasp the board about three-fourths of the way up the board. Do not lay on the board; your chest should be in the water. The kick board is a great tool for every level of swimming.

Pull-buoys are commonly used by swimmers to isolate the arm pull. The pull-buoy is a bi-cylinder floating device, held between your thighs to keep you from kicking, while providing buoyancy to your body's midsection. This extra buoyance makes it easier to swim and therefore enables you to concentrate on the arm pull. Once purchased, pull-buoys should last a lifetime.

▶ **Goggles**
Goggles are protective eye gear worn by swimmers.

▶ **Cap**
The cap is worn on the head in order to keep the hair out of the swimmer's face and protect the hair from chlorine.

▶ **Kick Board**
A kick board is used to isolate the swimmer's legs for a good workout. The kick board can also be used to help beginning swimmers float in the water.

▶ **Pull-buoy**
The pull-buoy is a bi-cylinder floating device, held between the thighs to inhibit kicking, while providing buoyancy to the body's midsection.

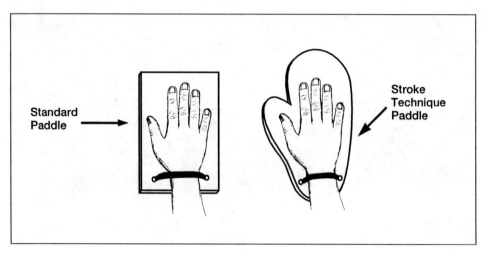

FIGURE 3-8 Two examples of paddles.

Training paddles are plastic hand paddles. They should extend slightly beyond your outstretched hand. The paddle increases the surface area of your hand, allowing you to pull more water and exaggerating the force of the arm pull. They can be used for conditioning or technical stroke work. Paddles are a more advanced training tool; overuse can cause shoulder stress. Again, once purchased, a set of paddles should last you for a lifetime of swimming.

Fins allow you to move through the water using your entire body in one fluid motion. They can be used for training or just for fun. Fins come in all shapes and sizes. The larger the fin, the more difficult it is to maneuver, and the more skill required.

SUMMARY

- In the United States, the 25-yard pool is the most common.
- At an indoor swimming pool you may find lane lines, a pace clock, backstroke flags, and starting blocks.
- A swimsuit, goggles, and a cap are the basic necessities to acquire before climbing into a pool to swim.

▶ **Training Paddles**
Plastic hand-held paddles that increase the surface area of your hand allowing you to pull more water.

CHAPTER 4

EXERCISES FOR THE
BEGINNING SWIMMER

Objectives

After reading this chapter, you should be able to do the following:

* Blow bubbles and breathe properly in the water.
* Float near the surface of the water.
* Kick in a prone position from the side of the pool.
* Practice the standing sculling drill and the advanced sculling drill.
* Perform the elementary backstroke.
* Push off the wall in the streamlined position.

KEY TERMS

While reading this chapter, you will become familiar with the following terms:

▶ **Flutter Kick**　　　　　　▶ **Streamlined Position**
▶ **Sculling**

FIGURE 4-1 Blowing bubbles.

The water is a great place to exercise, but it may take some getting used to. In this chapter are a few beginning tips to help you make the transition from dry land to water. The ultimate goal is to learn how to feel comfortable in the water. With some simple instruction you should be able to breathe, relax, and move around in the water with ease.

BLOWING BUBBLES

Exhaling under water is a key element to breathing while swimming. While standing or sitting in the shallow end of the pool, put your face in the water and blow bubbles until you have exhaled as much as you can. When you lift your face out of the water you are instantly ready to breathe in fresh oxygen. One way to practice this skill is to stand in the shallow end of the pool, and bob up and down in the water. Blow bubbles and all the air in your lungs out before coming up out of the water for your next breath. Exhale under the water, breathe in fresh air above the water.

FLOATING

While in the shallow end of the pool lie flat on your back with your head just out of the water. Take a big breath and relax in this position, floating near the surface of the water. The natural position your body will take is similar to sitting in a reclined chair completely stretched out. Breathe while you are floating. The more air you keep in your lungs the better you will float. Floating becomes easier the more relaxed the body becomes.

FIGURE 4-2 Floating.

KICKING IN THE PRONE POSITION FROM THE WALL

Grab the side of the pool with both hands. Stretch your body out into the prone position. Flutter kick into the wall. A **flutter kick** is the up and down motion of each foot kicking one at a time. Keep the kick small and

FIGURE 4-3 Two hands on the wall while kicking.

FIGURE 4-4 One hand on the wall while kicking.

rapid. Bend your knees only slightly while flutter kicking and point your toes. It is easier to flutter kick with relaxed ankles. During this exercise, work on proper breathing in the water. Place your head between your biceps, stretch out at the wall, exhale all your air, then turn your head to one side and take a breath. If you have trouble breathing to the side, practice breathing to the front.

After mastering this drill with both hands on the wall it is time to take the next step. With one hand remaining on the wall, place the other hand at your side. Rotate the shoulders and stretch out onto your side. Flutter kick and try to keep your entire body near the surface of the water. Practice breathing to the side.

You can do this exercise with the breaststroke kick as well. Assume the stretched out position with both hands on the wall. Pull your knees toward your chest, then point your toes out and in a whiplike fashion push your feet back together. This is the basic breaststroke kick, sometimes called the frog kick or whip kick. As with the flutter kick, try to keep your entire body close to the surface of the water.

STANDING SCULLING EXERCISE

Sculling is a key skill to develop in learning how to swim. Standing in the shallow end of the pool, place your arms in the water by your hips and practice mov-

▶ **Flutter Kick**

A flutter kick is the up and down motion of each foot kicking one at a time. Keep the kick small and rapid. Bend the knees only slightly while flutter kicking, and point the toes. This kick is used in freestyle and backstroke.

▶ **Sculling**

Moving the hands in and out in a figure eight, with palms facing the bottom of the pool, to propel the body through the water.

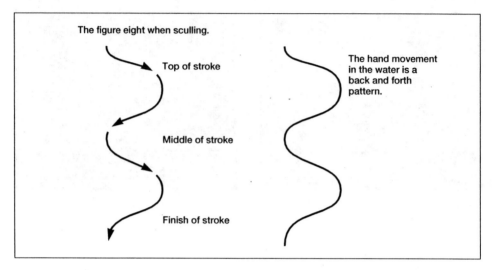

The figure eight when sculling.

Top of stroke

The hand movement in the water is a back and forth pattern.

Middle of stroke

Finish of stroke

FIGURE 4-5 Diagram of the figure-eight hand action when sculling.

FIGURE 4-6 The advanced scull position.

FIGURE 4-7 The floating scull.

ing your hands in and out in a figure-eight pattern with your palms facing the bottom of the pool. This is called sculling. Make sure the elbow is higher than the wrist in the water. When you are sculling properly you will feel your body being lifted up in the water by the sculling action.

ADVANCED SCULLING EXERCISE

Lift your legs off the bottom of the pool and pull them slightly toward your chest. Hold your head out of the water and scull. The buoyancy of the body and the sculling action suspends the body in the water. Try moving in all directions from this position.

The next step is to lie stretched out in the water, on your stomach or back, and scull to move your body around in the water.

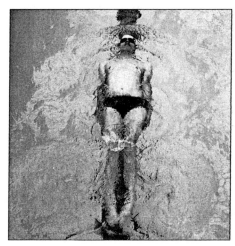

FIGURE 4-8 Elementary backstroke.

FIGURE 4-9 Elementary backstroke after the pull position.

ELEMENTARY BACKSTROKE

Lie flat on your back in the water with your hands at your sides. In one motion, bring your hands up above your head, keeping them in close to your body and under the water. At the same time bend your knees and bring your feet up toward your back. When your hands reach the stretched out position and your feet are up behind you, pull down with your arms and kick your feet back together. When you pull down with your arms remember to scull the water back and forth as you push the water toward your feet. Continue this action all the way down the pool. Watch out for the wall, and don't hit your head.

STREAMLINED POSITION PUSH

The **streamlined position** is one of the most important positions in swimming. The swimmer should pass through the water with the least amount of resistance

▶ **Streamlined Position**

A streamlined position is created by pushing off the wall with the arms and hands stretched out over the head. Place one hand over the other and squeeze the ears with the biceps. Point the toes and keep the feet close together. Hold the body as straight and tight as possible.

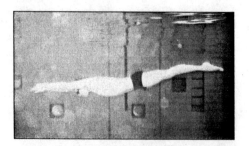

FIGURE 4-10 Streamlined position.

possible. The streamlined position is used off the start and off each wall. As a matter of fact, pushing off the wall in a streamlined fashion is the fastest a swimmer can travel through the water. A streamlined position is created by pushing off the wall with your arms and hands stretched out over your head. Place one hand over the other and squeeze your ears with your biceps. Point your toes and keep your feet close together. Hold your body as straight and tight as possible. This is the most efficient way to move through the water.

SUMMARY

- Blowing bubbles, floating, and kicking in the prone position from the wall are beginning techniques.
- Sculling is a key skill to develop in learning how to swim.
- A swimmer passes through the water with the least amount of resistance in the streamlined position.

CHAPTER 5

BASICS OF THE
FREESTYLE: TECHNIQUE

OBJECTIVES

After reading this chapter, you should be able to do the following:

- Demonstrate body position in the freestyle stroke.
- Recognize the importance of shoulder and hip rotation.
- Apply sculling to freestyle.
- Describe the basic freestyle stroke.
- Know how to start and turn in a freestyle race.

KEY TERMS

While reading this chapter, you will become familiar with the following terms:

- ► Recovery
- ► Two-beat Kick
- ► Six-beat Kick
- ► Stroke Drills

- ► Grab Start
- ► Track Start
- ► Flip Turn

FIGURE 5-1 Freestyle stroke in the stretch position.

FIGURE 5-2 Front view of freestyle at the waterline.

Freestyle is the fastest of the four strokes and the most widely used. It's the most versatile of all the strokes. A misleading description of freestyle conveys that swimmers swim on their stomachs. When swimming freestyle properly, you spend very little time on your stomach. Instead, you stretch out and rotate from side to side with each stroke.

The efficiency in moving through the water is of primary concern to any swimmer. We will start at the top of the stroke and work our way down to the kick.

FIGURE 5-3 Standing stretch.

HEAD POSITION

Head position is very important because the body will follow the head's lead. The head and face are pointed forward in the direction you are going. Your eyes should be just below the surface of the water.

While swimming freestyle, as with all of the strokes, it is important to keep the head still and straight. Excess movement of the head is inefficient. Proper head position keeps the body in a straight line.

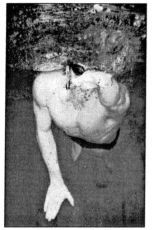  

FIGURES 5-4, 5-5, AND 5-6 Shoulder rotation during the freestyle.

SHOULDER AND HIP ROTATION

The body must stretch into position by extending one arm out over the head and rotating the shoulders and hips around the axis of the straight line maintained by the head. This stretch position is the same position one would use if he or she were trying to reach as high as possible with one hand. When reaching with one hand the shoulders rotate in order to get an extra couple inches of height.

The shoulders and hips rotate back and forth with each arm pull. By continually rotating, the swimmer actually spends very little time flat in the water.

SCULLING

Now that the body is in position, it is time to use the arms and hands as paddles to propel the body through the water. The motion your arms perform to accomplish this is called "sculling". Moving the pitch of the palm and forearm, in and out, under the water, creates the sculling action.

ARM PULL

The swimmer changes the pitch of the palm and forearm in and out throughout the pull, creating an "S" pattern in the stroke.

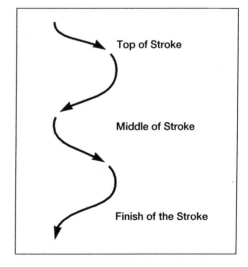

FIGURE 5-7 Diagram of the sculling motion—the figure eight.

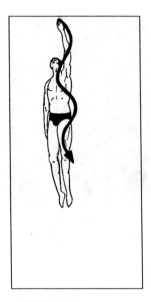

FIGURE 5-8 Diagram of the "S" pattern.

The freestyle arm pull can be broken down into four different sections: (1) the top of the stroke, (2) the middle, (3) the finish of the stroke, and (4) the recovery.

TOP OF STROKE

The top of the stoke is the entry of the hand into the water. The hand should enter the water with the thumb in line with your eyes, about 8 inches above the head. Apply pressure to the water as soon as the hand enters the water by rotating the shoulders and stretching into position. At this point, the hand is still out in front while the kick is propelling you forward and you are in a "body surfing" position. Now bend the elbow slightly making a small "scull" outward about 3 to 4 inches. Bend the elbow still further, bringing the hand back toward the middle of the body while maintaining a high elbow at all times.

MIDDLE OF STROKE

The middle of the stroke, under the body, is where you are applying the most strength and power to enhance forward movement. Maintaining a high elbow, scull inward to your belly button. This is the only time that the body is flat in the water. At this point the hand is directly under the belly button, and the shoulders are starting to rotate onto the other side.

FIGURE 5-9 Hand entry for the freestyle.

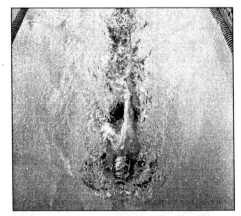

FIGURE 5-10 Body surfing position during the freestyle.

Performance Tip

The elbow should never be lower than the wrist. Flex your arm muscles with the elbow lower than the wrist. You will feel the flex in the biceps. Now raise the elbow above the wrist and flex. You will find the pressure of the flex has moved to your shoulders. The shoulders are stronger and therefore can help you move through the water easier.

FIGURE 5-11 Small scull.

FIGURE 5-12 The middle of the freestyle stroke.

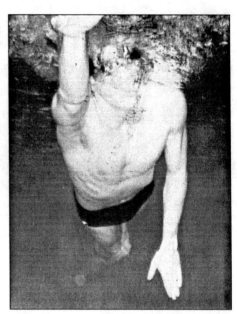

FIGURES 5-13 AND 5-14 Finish the stroke past the suit.

FINISH OF STROKE

The final scull is from the belly button out toward the hips, pushing the water behind your suit. The hand should not exit the water until you have pulled well past the suit. The thumb on the pulling hand should graze the thigh and you should apply pressure to the water all the way until the hand flips out of the water. The right arm pull should be at opposite position of the left arm pull at all times during the stroke. When the right hand is beginning to exit the water, the left hand is entering the water at the top of the stroke.

FIGURE 5-15 The stretch position. One hand is entering the water and the other hand is finishing the stroke.

RECOVERY

The last part of the stroke is the **recovery** where the arm moves through the air to reach the top of the next stroke. Bend the elbow and relax

FIGURE 5-16 Recovery of the freestyle stroke.

the forearm and hand. Bring the hand in as close to the body as possible as it moves to the top of the next stroke. The arm that is on the recovery needs to be as relaxed and fluid as possible.

KICK

The legs and feet are to be kept on the same plane as the head and body. The legs, ankles, and feet are rotating and kicking from side to side the same way the shoulders and hips rotate from side to side over the center axis. The kick should be small and fast. The feet should never separate more then 8 inches.

Kicking plays different roles depending on the distance you are swimming. Generally, there are two distinct styles of kick: the **two-beat kick** and the **six-beat kick**. The two-beat kick is one kick per arm pull. The six-beat kick is three kicks per arm pull. The two-beat kick is primarily used in distance events because it is easy to maintain over long distances. The six-beat kick is used for sprinting because of the greater power output.

BREATHING

Breathing is basic in all swimming events. Prepare to take a breath by exhaling all the air in your lungs while your face is in the water—before turning the head to breathe. This way you can bring in as much new oxygen in the short time you have when your mouth is out of the water.

▶ **Recovery**
The last part of the stroke where the arm moves through the air to reach the top of the next stroke.

▶ **Two-beat Kick**
The two-beat kick is one kick per arm pull.

▶ **Six-beat Kick**
The six-beat kick is three kicks per arm pull.

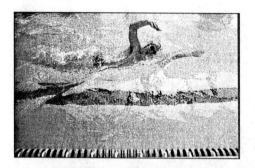

FIGURE 5-17 A swimmer taking a breath during the freestyle.

After exhaling, the breath is taken after the hand enters the water and the shoulders begin their rotation. As you stretch forward, rotating onto one side, turn your head to the opposite side (right arm stretch, breathing to the left). Tilt the head slightly allowing just the mouth to come out of the water. After taking in the breath, it is important to remember to put the head right back into the straight and forward position.

STROKE DRILLS

Stroke drills focus on one segment of the stroke and are often exaggerations of the stroke in order to overemphasize a particular section of the stroke. A good steady kick will enable you to maintain a good body position while working on stroke mechanics. Stroke drills should not be rushed, take your time.

1. **Drag finger tips:** This drill emphasizes keeping a high elbow on the recovery. While swimming normal freestyle, drag the fingertips across the surface of the water during the recovery of the stroke.
2. **Sculling drill:** This drill shows how powerful a tool sculling can be. This drill is done using the freestyle body position and moving through the water sculling only. Take no strokes and have no recovery. Simply move through the water by sculling at all three positions of the stroke.

THE FREESTYLE START

When a swimmer is comfortable enough to dive into the water off the starting blocks, there are two main styles to consider—the traditional **grab start** and the **track start**.

FIGURES 5-18 AND 5-19 Sculling motion.

FIGURE 5-20 Starting position for freestyle.

THE "GRAB" START

When the starter says "take your mark!" lean over quickly and assume the starting position. Place the feet hip width apart. Wrap the toes over the end of the block. Bend slightly at the knees and grab the block gently with your fingers.

Before leaving the block, try to point the toes and use the calf muscles to spring off the block. When the start is indicated, throw everything forward—the arms, head, hips all move forward in an out and down position. Just before entering the water bring the hands together and place your head between the biceps, stretch out the rest of the body and assume the streamlined position. Take advantage of the speed off the start by holding the streamlined position for at least one second. Then start to kick. As you come to the surface of the water, start the first pull and begin swimming.

THE TRACK START

The only difference in the track start is the position of the feet on the block. One foot remains at the front of the starting block, while the other foot is placed on the back of the block—similar to a track athlete starting a sprint race.

FREESTYLE TURNS

OPEN TURN

The most basic freestyle turn is the open turn. Swim to the wall and grab it with your hands. At the same time, pull the legs up to the chest and place the feet on the wall. The hand that is not touching the wall is left in the water. The hand touching

▶ **Stroke Drills**
These drills focus on one segment of the stroke and exaggerate it in order to overemphasize a particular section of the stroke.

▶ **Grab Start**
A start used off the block when the swimmer places both feet at the front of the block.

▶ **Track Start**
Starting off the block with one foot at the front of the block and one at the back of the block.

FIGURE 5-21 Off the block from the starting position.

FIGURE 5-22 Into the water after pushing off the block.

FIGURES 5-23, 5-24, AND 5-25 Open turn.

the wall is then brought over the head with a bent elbow, eventually meeting up with the opposite hand in the water. Pull the hands together while pushing off the wall in a streamlined fashion.

FLIP TURN

When executing the **flip turn,** swim close to the wall, but do not touch the wall with the hand. Instead tuck into a small ball and roll over in the water. At the end of the somersault the feet will be on the wall in position to push off in the other direction. Push off immediately. While you are pushing off the wall put your body in the streamlined position.

FREESTYLE FINISH

The freestyle should finish on your side in the stretch position, with the fingers extended. A strong kick into the wall will produce a faster finish.

FIGURES 5-26, 5-27, AND 5-28 Flip turn.

SUMMARY

- When swimming freestyle, good head position allows you to swim in a straight line.
- Shoulder rotation is emphasized along with sculling as two important aspects of the freestyle stroke. This chapter gives you ideas on how to have a more productive kick.
- The chapter ends with stroke drills and attention to details—the start, turns, and finishes.

FIGURE 5-29 Finish position for freestyle.

▶ **Flip Turn**

The swimmer swims as close to the wall, but does not touch the wall with the hand. Instead the swimmer tucks into a small ball and rolls over in the water. At the end of the somersault the feet will be on the wall in position to push off in the other direction.

CHAPTER 6

BASICS OF THE
BACKSTROKE: TECHNIQUE

OBJECTIVES

After reading this chapter, you should be able to do the following:

- Demonstrate proper head and body position while swimming the backstroke.
- Recognize similarities of backstroke and freestyle.
- Start a race with a backstroke start.

KEY TERMS

While reading this chapter, you will become familiar with the following terms:

▶ Recovery Portion of the Backstroke

▶ Backstroke Flags

The backstroke is very similar to freestyle except that the swimmer is swimming on the back. Backstroke is relaxing to swim because the face is out of the water all of the time, making it easy to breathe. Use this stroke of choice for warm up and warm down to ease your breathing.

HEAD POSITION

The head position is backstroke keeps the body in a straight line. Swimming in a straight line is important in backstroke considering you are not looking toward the direction you are swimming. Your head should be on the water's surface, looking toward the feet. Do not tuck the chin down into the neck, but keep the chin forced out and up. A good head position can help keep your body on top of the water.

FIGURE 6-1 Head position in the backstroke.

BODY POSITION

Body position is also very important in backstroke. You must arch the back and make sure that the chest is out of the water. Strong kicking will help maintain a good body position. When the kick becomes weak, the rear end sags in the water, eventually pulling the chest down in the water. The body position needs to be flat and streamlined.

SHOULDER ROTATION

The shoulders rotate off the axis of the chin and sternum of the chest. Each shoulder should rotate to the point that it grazes the chin. Remember do not take the chin to the shoulder, but take each shoulder to the chin. The hips will rotate naturally with the shoulders. Standing on a flat surface and rotating the shoulders shows the natural rotation of the hips. The shoulder rotation gives you an advantage when trying to perform the stroke.

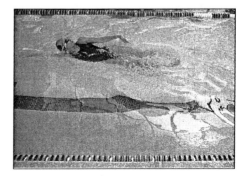

THE STROKE PATTERN

As with freestyle there are four sections of one arm stroke: (1) the entry, (2) the middle, (3) the finish, and (4) the recovery.

FIGURE 6-2 Body position in the backstroke.

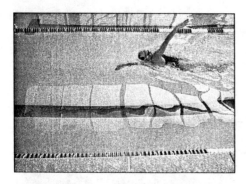

FIGURE 6-3 Shoulder rotation in the backstroke.

FIGURE 6-4 Hand entry during the backstroke.

ENTRY OF STROKE

The entry of the hand into the water should be "pinky first". The hand should enter, arm stretched out, at the 1 o'clock position. Entering with the pinky positions the hand properly to apply pressure to the water immediately. This is the body surfing position of the backstroke which is similar to freestyle. As the hand enters the water "pinky first," drive the hand down as far as possible with the aid of the rotating shoulder. This will help you grab deep stationary water.

MIDDLE OF STROKE

The middle of the stroke is highlighted by bending the elbow immediately following the deep drive of the entry approximately 8 to 12 inches under the water. Bending the elbow will bring the hand closer to the surface of the water. The hand should not break the surface of the water, but pull the water 3 to 5 inches below the surface. This is the middle of the stroke, still above the suit.

FINISH OF STROKE

At the finish of the stroke, the hand will come close to the body at the hip. At this point the hand and the wrist throw the water down toward the feet forcibly. The stronger the finish of the stroke the easier it will be to drive the opposite stroke deep at the entry of the next stroke. A strong finish to the midpoint of the thigh will also aid your shoulder rotation.

RECOVERY

Following a strong finish of the stroke, the arm will need to be swung through the air and back to the top of the stroke. This is the **recovery portion of the back-**

FIGURE 6-5 Middle of the backstroke.

FIGURE 6-6 Finish of the backstroke.

stroke. In backstroke, the recovery is straight-armed. As the hand starts its downward motion you need to be thinking of the entry, twisting the hand in position for a pinky first entry.

Many swimmers have problems with the recovery in backstroke. One problem is the tendency to bend the elbow while the hand is in the air. If you bend the elbow on recovery it will flatten out the shoulders and work against the rotation. The second problem is forgetting to twist the wrist before the entry, causing you to slap the water and pause the stroke.

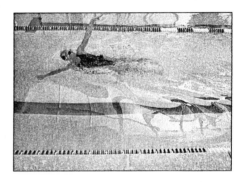

FIGURE 6-7 Recovery portion of the backstroke.

THE KICK

The backstroke kick is a small fast kick, which does not break the streamlined position of the body. A strong consistent kick will hold the body closer to the surface of the water. The kick should be small, not allowing the feet to separate more than 8 inches. Resist the tendency to bend the knees too much. The ideal position for the knees is just under the surface of the water.

BREATHING

Breathing while swimming backstroke is easier than in other strokes because your face is out of the water. The most important aspect of

▶ **Recovery Portion of the Backstroke**
Following a strong finish of the stroke, the arm will need to be swung through the air and back to the top of the stroke.

breathing is to find a rhythm that suits you. There is no set time in the stroke when you should breathe. However, it is important to breathe a lot. The more you breathe, the more oxygen gets to the muscles and, therefore, you will have more strength and experience less fatigue.

STROKE DRILLS

1. Single-arm backstroke: This drill is as it sounds. Swim backstroke for one length using only the right arm. This drill is designed to increase shoulder rotation awareness. While the right arm is pulling, the left shoulder should lift up to the chin. Keep the head and body straight, even though you are only using one arm. Take time and concentrate on the stroke not on how fast you are going. Repeat this on the next length using the left arm.
2. Two-arm backstroke: Swim backstroke using both arms at the same time. This drill is designed to work on the underwater pull of the stroke and balancing the stroke. Swim down the pool, pulling with both arms and using a normal backstroke kick. Drive both arms deep and bend the elbows simultaneously and finish strong with both pulls. Keep the head straight and try to swim in a straight line.

BACKSTROKE START

Only practice your starts in deep water.

STARTING POSITION

The backstroke competition starts in the water from the side of the pool. Reach up and find a comfortable place to grab the block—mainly on the bar that goes across the front of the block or the edge of the pool. After finding a good place for

FIGURE 6-8 Backstroke starting position.

FIGURE 6-9 Off the blocks from the starting position.

FIGURE 6-10 Backstroke approach.

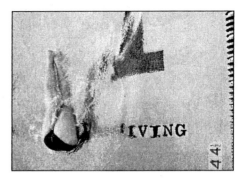

FIGURE 6-11 Flip turn.

the hands, place the feet about 4 to 6 inches under the surface of the water. Plant the feet on the wall hip width apart.

When the starter commands, "Take your mark!", pull up with your arms slightly. When the start is signaled, push off with the legs and hands at the same time. Arch the back drastically and throw the arms above your head. Pull the body together in a streamlined position before entering the water.

Once you enter the water, hold the streamlined position for one second, then start to kick. The kick can be a regular flutter kick or a dolphin kick. Rules dictate that backstroke swimmers cannot go farther than 15 yards/meters under the water at the beginning of the race or off of any turn.

BACKSTROKE TURN

The backstroke turn is similar to the freestyle flip turn. You are allowed to take one freestyle arm pull prior to starting the turn. Then tuck into a small ball and somersault over, making it a freestyle turn with one subtle difference.

In backstroke, you need to count the strokes it takes to get from the **backstroke flags**, to the point where you roll over and take the freestyle stroke. The backstroke flags are flags hung across the pool 5 yards from the end of each wall. They are used to give a warning that you are approaching the wall.

When pushing off the wall pull into a streamlined position and stay on the back. Flutter kick or dolphin kick until you pop onto the surface of the water, before the 15 yard/meter mark.

BACKSTROKE FINISH

Stay on your back until you touch the wall. Swim into the wall making sure you know how many strokes it takes to swim from the

▶ **Backstroke Flags**

The backstroke flags are flags hung across the pool 5 yards from the end of each wall. They are used to give a warning that the swimmer is approaching the wall.

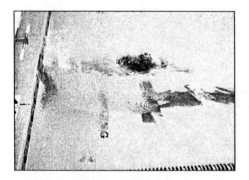

FIGURE 6-12 The backstroker pulls into a streamlined position.

FIGURE 6-13 The backstroke finish.

backstroke flags to the wall. Throw one arm to the finish, rotating the shoulder to get maximum stretch. Then finish with the tips of the finger, stretched out on your side.

SUMMARY

- Many of the same skills, from head position to shoulder rotation, used in freestyle are also performed in backstroke.
- Stroke drills play an important part in learning proper technique.

CHAPTER 7

BASICS OF THE
BREASTSTROKE: TECHNIQUE

OBJECTIVES

After reading this chapter, you should be able to do the following:

- Demonstrate the correct positioning and understand the fundamentals of the breaststroke.
- Perform an underwater pull out.

KEY TERMS

While reading this chapter, you will become familiar with the following terms:

▶ **Frog Kick**   ▶ **Underwater Pull Out**

▶ **Whip Kick**

The breaststroke is a great stroke to swim and one of the oldest strokes. The breaststroke is the slowest of all strokes because the recovery for the arm pull is under the water. Therefore, it is important to keep the stroke long and thin, imagining yourself trying to swim through the smallest cylinder possible.

HEAD POSITION

The stroke starts in the streamlined position. The hands are stretched out over the head with the head tucked between both bicep muscles. The head becomes more of a driving force in the breaststroke. You begin to lift the head up and out of the water at the beginning of the stroke. The head lifts forcefully enough to lift the shoulders and back up and out of the water. You breathe and then drive the head back down at the completion of the stroke cycle, back into the streamlined position. By driving the head down onto the water you help keep body and hips closer to the surface of the water.

BODY POSITION

The body position in breaststroke starts and finishes in the streamlined position. The entire body should remain close to the water's surface. Remember to keep the body in a small cylinder, straight and flat in the water. Try not to let the hips and legs sink lower than the chest. When the arm pull is taken, the back arches out of the water, literally trying to lift the whole body out of the water. The body action along with the head movement helps keep the body on top of the water.

THE STROKE PATTERN

From the streamlined position, press down on the water with your hands and scull out to the width of the shoulders. Bend the elbows, keeping the elbows higher than the wrists at all times, and start the inward scull back to the middle of the body. When you pull back toward your body do not bring the arms all the way back into your chest or ribs. Keep the arms out in front of the chest and bring the elbows together. While bringing the elbows together shrug your shoulders to aid in lifting the back up out of the water. At this point your hands are directly under your head and at the water's surface. This is when the breath is taken.

FIGURE 7-1 Head position in the breaststroke.

FIGURE 7-2 Body position in the breaststroke.

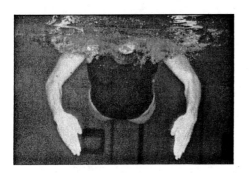

FIGURE 7-3 Stroke pattern of the breaststroke.

FIGURE 7-4 Position in the breaststroke when the breath is taken.

RECOVERY

The recovery in breaststroke is actually a lunge forward with the hands, arms, and head. Hold the hands close together while pushing them forward on the surface of the water. If the recovery takes place too far under the surface of the water, you will create more drag and become inefficient in the water. The recovery, or lunge forward, is motivated by the whip action of the kick.

FIGURE 7-5 Recovery in the breaststroke.

THE KICK

The kick in the breaststroke is referred to as a frog kick or whip kick. The jumping or lunging forward action with each kick resembles that of a frog—hence the name **frog kick**. The **whip kick** is so named because of the whipping action of the legs as they come together at the end of the kick.

From the streamlined position, start the pull and at the same time bend the knees and bring both feet up the buttocks. Allow the knees to spread out as far as

▶ **Frog Kick**
The kicking in the breaststroke is referred to as a frog kick because the swimmer is jumping or lunging forward with each kick.

▶ **Whip Kick**
A breaststroke kick that generates propulsion by the whipping action of the legs coming back together at the end of the kick.

Fitness Tip

The Stroke Sequence

- The swimmer starts in the streamlined position.
- Simultaneously, the swimmer takes the arm pull and brings the feet up to the buttocks.
- The legs kick at the same time as the arms, head, and shoulders are lunging forward. After this motion the swimmer's body goes back to the streamlined position.

the shoulders. When the feet have reached the buttocks, flex the ankles and point the feet out toward the side of the pool. This creates the most surface area for the feet, allowing the feet to grab more water. With the toes pointed out, whip the feet back together and squeeze them together tight. Now you are in the streamlined position and ready to take the next stroke.

STROKE DRILLS

1. **Lunging drill:** Push off the wall in a streamlined position. Take a normal breaststroke pull, but concentrate on lunging forward with your hands, head, and arms on the recovery. At the same time, try to get the most power out of your kick that you can. After each lunge forward return to the streamlined position and glide. Try to glide farther with every lunge.
2. **Take a Stroke Off drill:** This drill is very simple but a great tool for learning to swim breaststroke more efficiently. Swim one length of breaststroke at your normal speed. Count the number of strokes it takes you to get from one

FIGURES 7-6 and 7-7 The kick in the breaststroke.

FIGURE 7-8 The breaststroke turn approaching the wall.

FIGURE 7-9 Pull knees into the chest.

end to the other. Then swim the next length with one fewer stroke. Practice swimming the length with as few strokes as possible. This drill forces you to get maximum power out of every stroke.

BREASTSTROKE START

The breaststroke start is the same as the freestyle grab or track start, except you are allowed one full stroke and kick under the water called the **underwater pull out.** You are allowed this at the start of the race and off of each wall or turn, while moving under the water in the streamlined position. Then you take a breaststroke pull but continue the pull with both arms all the way down to the thighs. Bring the feet up to the buttocks and, at the same time, bring the hands up to the front of the stroke, keeping the hands in close to the body.

Take one breaststroke kick. The kick will need to propel you up to the surface of the water. Just before you reach the surface of the water, you should be in the streamlined position. When the head breaks the surface of the water begin the normal stroke pattern.

BREASTSTROKE TURN

Approach the wall in a stretched out position. Touch the wall with both hands parallel. Pull the knees into the chest, forcing one arm into the body under the water. While the other arm has a bent elbow, it reaches over the head and out of the water. Place the feet even with the hips on the wall. Both hands will meet over the head and begin to stretch into the streamlined position. Explode off the wall using the leg muscles and hold the streamlined position for at least one second. Then start the underwater pull out.

▶ **Underwater Pull Out**

The breaststroker is allowed one full stroke cycle and kick underwater at the start of the race and off of each wall or turn.

FIGURE 7-10 Explode off the wall with the feet.

FIGURE 7-11 Hold the streamlined position.

BREASTSTROKE FINISH

Swim to the wall and finish with both arms stretched out in front. Lunge for the wall with the final stroke.

The breaststroke is a terrific stroke to swim at any speed. Breathing is easy and consistent. The coordination and strength it takes to swim fast can be very challenging and exciting.

SUMMARY

• Breaststroke is the slowest of all the strokes because the arm recovery is underwater.

FIGURE 7-12 The breaststroke finish.

• Due to the mandatory recovery style, it is important to move through the water keeping your body's movements within as small a cylinder as possible. Do this by pulling your body into a streamlined position after every stroke, and by keeping your elbows and knees inside the width of your shoulders.

• The lunge is an important part of swimming breaststroke properly.

CHAPTER 8

BASICS OF THE
BUTTERFLY: TECHNIQUE

OBJECTIVES

After reading this chapter, you should be able to do the following:

• Understand the importance of undulating in butterfly.
• Know the basic techniques of the butterfly.

KEY TERMS

While reading this chapter, you will become familiar with the following terms:

► Undulation   ► Dolphin Kick

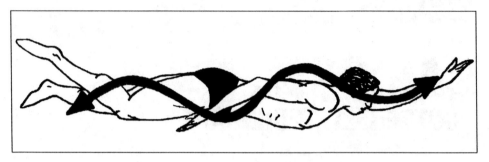

FIGURE 8-1 Undulate—move like a snake or fish through the water.

The butterfly is the most difficult of all the strokes to swim at any speed. Done right, however, it can be the most beautiful of all strokes. The fact that both arms are out of the water at the same time during the recovery of the stroke makes the butterfly difficult to perform. The body becomes the main engine and must undulate like a fish to propel you through the water. The **undulation** is a wavelike movement of the body, which moves the swimmer forward in the water. The arms will work in conjunction with this undulating motion.

HEAD POSITION

The head position in butterfly is actually a movement. The head is used to start the first wavelike motion as well as to breathe. The head position while breathing should be face forward with the chin jutting outward on the surface of the water. When you are not inhaling, the head should drive down just under the water's surface to start the movement of the stroke and the first undulation of the body. Breathing every stroke helps maintain good body undulation.

Performance Tip

The butterflyer is trying to imitate a fish. The fish has no arms or legs but moves through the water with the greatest of ease. Similar to the way a fish moves back and forth in the water in order to move forward in a straight line, the butterflyer is attempting to do the same.

FIGURES 8-2 AND 8-3 Head position in the butterfly.

BODY POSITION

In the butterfly, the body becomes an engine and therefore it is not simply a matter of body position. As with the other strokes, it is important to keep the entire body from head to toes near the surface of the water. When the head dips down, the chest will follow a similar downward motion. Pull your chest back up to the surface by arching the back. The hips will follow the chest in the water. Consciously push your hips up to the surface of the water. The hip movement flows down to the kick, connecting the stroke into one complete body stroke. The body moves fluidly and the kick becomes the tail end of the stroke.

THE STROKE PATTERN

The arms should work in conjunction with the undulation of the body and not against it.

HAND ENTRY AND TOP OF STROKE

The stroke starts in the stretch or streamlined position. Both hands enter the water at the same time and about 2 inches apart. Do not cross the hands over each other.

When your head is about to start the upward undulation, start to pull a small outward scull. As the chest starts to move forward and up, widen the outward scull. The first scull is out to the width of the shoulders.

▶ **Undulation**

A wavelike movement of the body, which moves the swimmer forward in the water. The arms will work in conjunction with this undulating motion.

FIGURE 8-4 Body position in the butterfly.

FIGURE 8-5 Stroke entry for the butterfly.

FIGURE 8-6 First scull in the butterfly.

FIGURE 8-7 Pull under the body.

FIGURE 8-8 Recovery portion of the butterfly.

MIDDLE OF STROKE

As the hands push out farther than the shoulders, bend the elbows and start the inward scull. The hands should be directly under the center of the body. Start to take the breath at this time. The hands should meet at the belly button.

FINISH OF STROKE

The final sculling action is out and down past the hips. A rule of thumb is to swipe the thumb across the thigh to emphasize the finish of the stroke.

RECOVERY

The recovery in butterfly is the most difficult of all the strokes because both arms are out of the water at the same time. As the arms pull out of the water, bend the elbows, keeping the hands close to the surface of the water.

THE DOLPHIN KICK

This kick applies pressure to the water in two directions—up and down. Both legs *must* move together simultaneously. If the legs separate it is an illegal kick. Keep both feet together and the toes pointed. The kick becomes like a dolphin's tail moving up and down in the water to achieve forward motion. This is where the term **dolphin kick** comes from.

A trick to a good butterfly is to kick twice during the stroke. The first kick is taken at the beginning of the stroke, at the same time the head is forcing down to start the undulation. The upward sweep helps the hips drive forward and keeps the body undulating with force. This second smaller, faster kick, helps the body stay on top of the water and should be taken at the finish of the stroke. A quick undulation from the hips to the toes gives the body one more kick at the end of the stroke, which will allow the body to stay on top of the water.

BREATHING

The breath is taken during the last scull out to the thighs—at the very end of the stroke just before the recovery. The chin is lifted to the surface of the water and the breath is taken.

► **Dolphin Kick**

Both legs must move together simultaneously. If the legs separate, the swimmer is performing an illegal kick. Keep both feet together and the toes pointed. The kick becomes like a dolphin's tail moving up and down in the water propelling the swimmer forward.

FIGURES 8-9 and 8-10 Fly breathing.

Butterflyer's breathe directly to the front with the face forward. Breathing every stroke or every other stroke are the most common breathing patterns.

STROKE DRILLS

1. **Practice Undulating:** Lie flat in the water on your stomach with both arms at your sides. Dip the head down and forward and then back up to the surface. Dipping the head should make the rest of the body react in a undulating fashion. Next, use all the muscles in the body to emphasize the undulation movement, start with the head, then the chest, hips, and legs. This will move you forward in the water.
2. **Dolphin Kick on the Side:** Dolphin kick is the name given to the kick in butterfly because of the resemblance to a dolphin's taillike movement. This is a very simple drill, which helps you develop a better undulation. In this drill lie on your side in the water with both arms at your sides. Simply undulate and dolphin kick all the way down the pool. Practice swimming in a straight line.
3. **One-arm Butterfly:** Practice swimming butterfly with one arm, continuing to undulate the body and breathing to the front as if you were swimming with both arms. During this drill, stretch the resting arm out in front of the body. This will help balance your drill.

FIGURE 8-11 Fly turn in the butterfly.

THE BUTTERFLY START

The butterfly start is the same as the freestyle grab or track start except for the kick. After entering the pool, you must use the dolphin kick.

BUTTERFLY TURN

You must touch the wall with both hands on the same plane before turning around and going the other way. Approach the wall in a stretched out position. Touch the wall with both hands parallel. Pull the knees into the chest. One arm is forced into the body under the water. The other arm, with the elbow bent, reaches over the head and out of the water. Place the feet even with the hips on the wall. Both hands meet over the head stretched into the streamlined position. Explode off the wall using the leg muscles and hold the streamlined position for at least one second. Then start the undulation and the dolphin kick.

BUTTERFLY FINISH

The butterflyer swims to the wall and finishes with both arms stretched out in front dolphin kicking all the way into the wall.

SUMMARY

- The butterfly is the most difficult stroke to learn, but once you start using your entire body to move through the water like a fish you will master the stroke.
- The key to the butterfly stroke is the undulating movement of the body. Once this is mastered, the arm strokes, breathing, and kick will be easier to perform.

CONDITIONING ON
DRY LAND

OBJECTIVES

After reading this chapter, you should be able to do the following:

- Perform basic individual stretches.
- Assist a partner with basic stretches.

KEY TERMS

While reading this chapter, you will become familiar with the following terms:

- ▶ **Standing Stretch Position**
- ▶ **Figure Eight Stretch**
- ▶ **Wind Mill Stretch**

- ▶ **Scapula Stretch**
- ▶ **Partner Stretching**

Stretching plays an important part in all sports and swimming is no exception. Swimming in an easy manner is itself a form of stretching. There are some specific stretches, however, that swimmers can do to prepare for exercise sessions. Stretching can be done with a partner or on an individual basis. Stretching before you swim will create better blood flow for the body and loosen up tendons and muscles. Swimmers should stretch before every workout or competition.

FIGURE 9-1 Standing stretch position.

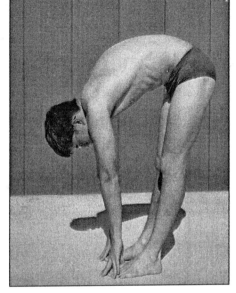

FIGURE 9-2 Stretch—touch toes.

Relax and breathe during your stretching routine. Take time in between stretches and focus on how the body is reacting to the stretching exercises. One way to stay relaxed and focused is to start most of the stretching exercises from the same position.

INDIVIDUAL STRETCHING

THE STANDING STRETCH POSITION

The **standing stretch position** consists of standing up straight, feet hip width apart, relaxing the knees and pushing the pelvis forward slightly. All standing stretches should be conducted from this position. In the beginning you might have to remind yourself to breathe and relax the knees.

TOUCH TOES

This is an old, but important, stretch. Lean over and reach for the toes. Once the body feels the stretch in the legs or back, stop, take a deep breath and hold for 7 seconds. Use

▶ **Standing Stretch Position**
All standing stretches can be conducted from this position—feet hip width apart, relaxed knees, slightly forward thrust of the pelvis.

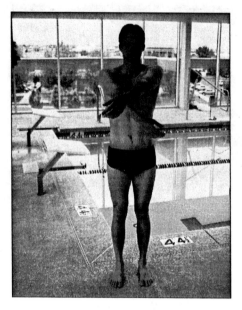 

FIGURES 9-3 and 9-4 Figure eight stretch.

the weight of the shoulders and the head to aid the stretch. DO NOT BOUNCE. When coming back up to the standing position keep the chin in tight to the body. This keeps the backbone straight. Repeat this three times. You should be able to get closer to your toes with every stretch.

FIGURE EIGHTS

Doing the **figure eight stretch** loosens up the shoulders. Swing the shoulders and arms in front of the body and then back behind the body; do not take the arms above the shoulders. This stretch loosens up the top of the shoulders and is a preparation stretch for the wind mills.

WIND MILLS

The **wind mill stretch** is probably the most popular swimming stretch. Swing the arms in big full

FIGURE 9-5 Wind mill stretch.

FIGURE 9-6 Triceps stretch #1.

FIGURE 9-7 Triceps stretch #2.

circles both forward and backward above the shoulders. This loosens up the shoulders and all the tendons and muscles around the shoulder. Rotate the arms slowly. Even the simplest of stretches can hurt the body. This stretch should be avoided if any shoulder problems exist.

TRICEPS STRETCH #1

The triceps are well used in swimming. In the standing stretch position, grab the left elbow with the right forearm and stretch the left elbow and arm across the chest. Repeat with the opposite arm. Every stretch should be done slowly and easily.

TRICEPS STRETCH #2

From the standing position, raise one arm above the head and drop the forearm and hand down behind the middle of the head and neck. Reach up with the opposite hand and pull the elbow up and toward the middle of the head. Stay balanced on this stretch.

▶ **Figure Eight Stretch**
Good stretch to loosen up the shoulders. Swing the shoulders and arms in front of the body and then back behind the body.

▶ **Wind Mill Stretch**
Swing the arms in big full circles both forward and backward above the shoulders.

SCAPULA STRETCH

To perform the **scapula stretch,** clasp the hands together and reach out in front as far as possible. This stretches the middle of the upper back. Then fold the hands and forearms over and stretch out again. You should notice this stretch on the top of the shoulders and the upper middle portion of the back.

ANKLE STRETCH

Sit on your ankles with your feet under your buttocks and your toes pointed behind you. Sitting in this position will help create better ankle flexibility.

PARTNER STRETCHING

Partner stretching can be more efficient if there is clear communication between partners when stretching. A simple hand gesture is all that is needed. A verbal gesture is hard to produce in some stretching positions. Therefore, the person who is stretching should simply indicate to the partner by wiggling the fingers. Be aware of your partner's communications.

FIGURE 9-8 Scapula stretch.   **FIGURE 9-9** Ankle stretch.

PARTNER SHOULDER STRETCH #1

Stand behind the person being stretched. Your partner extends straight arms behind the back as far as possible. Grab both wrists and pull them together, slowly. When your partner feels the stretch he or she wiggles the fingers. Hold the arms in this position for 7 seconds. Then release the arms and your partner relaxes for a few seconds before the stretch is performed again.

Communication between partners is essential. Stretching partners should be reminding each other to breathe and relax the knees. No pain or discomfort should be associated with stretching. In this stretch a partner may want to grab just above the elbows in order to take the pressure off a sore elbow.

FIGURE 9-10 Partner shoulder stretch #1.

PARTNER SHOULDER STRETCH #2

Stand behind your partner. Your partner places the palms of the hands on the back of his or her hips and brings the elbows toward the middle of the back. Grab the elbows with open palms and pull the arms together toward the center of the back, slowly. When your partner's fingers wiggle, hold the position for 7 seconds then release and allow your partner to relax the arms. Repeat the process twice.

LOWER BACK AND LEGS

Sit on the floor with your legs straight out in front, knees slightly bent. Reach down toward the toes. Your partner lightly pushes on your back. When you

▶ **Scapula Stretch**
Clasp the hands together and reach out front as far as possible.

▶ **Partner Stretching**
Allows for one person to apply resistance on another person when stretching before a workout.

FIGURE 9-11 Partner shoulder stretch #2.

FIGURE 9-12 Lower back stretch.

wiggle your fingers, your partner holds the position for 7 seconds. Return to the sitting position and take a big breath. Repeat two more times.

SUMMARY

- Stretching has always been an important aspect of sports training and swimming is no exception.
- This chapter covers the basic individual stretching exercises, as well as a few partner stretches.
- These stretches focus on the shoulders, legs, and back, all of which need to be loose and warm before getting into the water. Remember to stretch gently and breathe deeply.

WORKOUT SCHEDULES: VITAL TO FITNESS

OBJECTIVES

After reading this chapter, you should be able to do the following:

- Know how to circle swim.
- Properly perform a warm up and warm down routine.
- Plan a workout session.
- Manipulate your own workout by descending or building and using intervals.

KEY TERMS

While reading this chapter, you will become familiar with the following terms:

▶ Dry Land Exercises

▶ Circle Swimming

▶ Warm Up

▶ Interval Training

▶ Descending Set

▶ Build Set

▶ Negative Split Set

▶ Warm Down

▶ Feel for the Water

▶ Taper

▶ Yardage

GETTING STARTED IN THE SPORT OF SWIMMING

In this chapter we will cover the basics of swimming etiquette and terminology, workout strategy, and seasonal strategies. Using swimming as a main source of fitness is wonderful if you have access to a pool year-round. If not, or in addition to swimming for fitness, you can utilize **dry land exercises** and stretching. Dry land exercises are what swimmers call anything they would do outside the water. (For example: jogging, weight lifting, calisthenics, etc.). If exercising time is limited you might want to stretch and do the dry land work at home. Stretching each day is great for increasing flexibility.

When swimming in any venue you should know how to circle swim. **Circle swimming** is a simple solution to creating more room for three or more swimmers swimming in one lane at the same time. The swimmer simply swims down the right-hand side of the lane in both directions. Unless of course the swimmer is swimming in England or Australia where they swim on the left side. This prevents swimmers from colliding with each other. You should choose a lane with swimmers of comparable speed and ability.

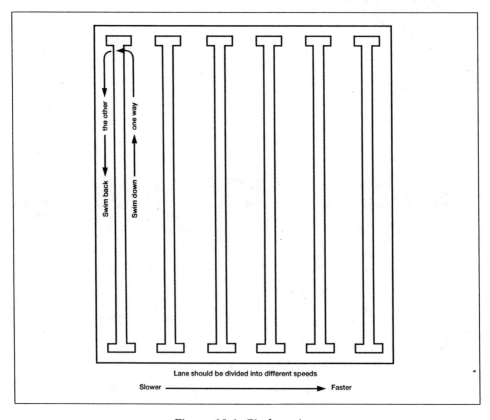

Figure 10-1 Circle swim.

YOUR FITNESS SESSION

Training sessions are designed and categorized into three basic sections. You will start off easy with a warm up, gradually increase in intensity and difficulty to a main set, then ease off and eventually wind up the workout with a warm down.

WARM UP

The **warm up** should be very easy, slow, and with a perfect stroke. All strokes may be used in warm up except butterfly, which is seldom used. The warm up should make up at least 20 percent of the total workout and many coaches and swimmers will do about 33 percent of their workout in the warm up mode. Easy does it.

MAIN SET

The rest of the workout will be based on **interval training**. Interval training is swimming a certain distance on a prescribed send-off time. (for example, 10 x 50 swim on the 1:00 minute). The 1:00 minute is the interval for that set and you swim 50 yards ten times leaving every 1:00 minute. This means that if you finish on the :43 then you rest until the clock reaches 1:00 minute. At which point you start the second 50 yards. You will need to use a pace clock or your own wristwatch to time your intervals. The interval allows you time to rest after each 50 yards. The main set should be about one-third of the total workout.

▶ **Different Styles of Main Sets**

There are many ways a swimmer can swim the main set or the distances within the set. **Descending set** refers to the whole set, for example in the 10 x 50 swim, descend on

▶ **Dry Land Exercises**
Exercises performed outside the water such as jogging, weight lifting, calisthenics, etc.

▶ **Circle Swimming**
Creating more room for three or more swimmers swimming in one lane at the same time. The swimmer simply swims down the right-hand side of the lane, both directions.

▶ **Warm Up**
The warm up should be very easy, slow, and with a perfect stroke. All the strokes can be used in warm up except butterfly, which is seldom used.

▶ **Interval Training**
Used for a swimmer to do sets on a prescribed set of time. For example 10 x 50 swim on the 1:00 minute. The 1:00 minute is the interval for that set, and a swimmer would swim 50 yards ten times leaving every 1:00 minute.

▶ **Descending Set**
During a descending set the swimmer is expected to start the first 50 at an easy pace and then go a little faster on each 50, with the last one being the fastest.

the 1:00. You start the first 50 yards at an easy pace and then go a little faster on each 50 yards with the last one being the fastest. Exert about a 10 percent increase in effort over the set.

A **build set**, as it refers to the 50s in the 10 x 50 set would be a set read; 10 x 50 build on the 1:00. You would start each 50 easy and build up the speed within the fifty finishing each 50 yards fast. You would be building each 50 about the same time. Another option is to **negative split** the 50s. If the set is a 10 x 50 swim, negative split on the 1:00. You would negative split each 50 by swimming the second half of the 50 faster than the first half.

The main set might be a quality set. In a quality set you get enough rest in between the fast swims to actually give 85 percent effort or above on all the required fast swims. For example, the set would read 10 x 50 fast on 3-5-7 and 10 on the 3:00. Make sure the rest is long enough to recover from the previous fast 50 yards . In this particular set you are expected to go all out on 3-5-7-10.

A short rest set is where you would go fast on each 50 yards and get limited rest. Generally no more than 5 seconds. The set would read 5 x 50 on the :40. At this interval you should be going around :35 seconds per every fifty yards. Obviously the interval will change depending on your swimming ability and speed.

These variations of the same set work on different aspects of swimming. The quality set works on your speed. While the short rest set works on your endurance. The build set helps you swim faster but with a good stroke. You should pay attention to the stroke while building momentum. When you increase the effort, a good stroke will be maintained. The negative split works on endurance. The swimmer is trying to go the second half of the distance faster than the first.

WARM DOWN

Before you call it a day of exercising in the pool you should **warm down**. The warm down is an easy swim similar to the warm up. This easy swimming works the fatigue out of the muscles. This is done by simply swimming easy at the end of every work-out. The warm down should comprise at least 10 percent of the work-out period.

KICKING DURING TRAINING

It is essential to do at least 20 percent of the training kick. Some swimmers will do up to 30 percent kick. Considering that the kick is a major force in all strokes it is wise to pay attention to the kick sets.

FROM A COMPETITIVE SWIMMER'S PERSPECTIVE: THE SEASON

Each season is divided into three basic sections: the over distance, the specialty, and the taper.

During the over distance section of the season you are getting back into shape. Therefore, the swim sets are long and focused on easy intervals. The over distance training is needed in order to gain a **feel for the water**. A feel for the water occurs when you can feel the effect each sculling motion has on the water, and can, at will, change the effort and speed at each section of the scull. Some swimmers seem to do this naturally, while others need a great deal of practice. Either way, in the beginning of the season it is hard to get a feel for the water. So you need to do a lot of swimming. This is why it is called the "over distance" part of the season. There is very little pressure for you to swim fast on the long sets. Actually you will want to maintain a comfortable speed to avoid stressing the shoulders and causing problems. Training too hard and too fast at the beginning of the season will put you at risk of shoulder problems. For the most part you should swim long, easy yardage for the first one-third of the season.

The specialty phase is comprised of some over distance work and training specifically related to the event that you will swim in races. Specifically, the swim sets, kick sets, and the stroke drills are geared toward your best stroke. The reason it is called specialty is because you are doing more specific types of training and not as much easy swimming.

The **taper** is the most mentally challenging phase of the season. It is the time of the season when you will gradually cut back on the amount of yardage in a workout. **Yardage** is the distance covered in the entire training session. After working hard all year long, chronic fatigue sets into the muscles. The taper will let the muscles recover. Theoretically the muscles are stronger than before when you were swimming much more yardage. This is because muscles heal during the taper and will actually heal to the point where they are stronger than before the taper.

This is done in hopes that you will feel fresh, strong, and ready to swim fast at the end of the season. If you do not taper for a meet at the end of the season you would probably have a good meet. But if you want to have a great meet you will need to be rested for it and tapered. How long you taper and what you do over the taper will depend on the age, strength, and swimming event.

The taper can also be the most difficult time of the year for you

▶ **Build Set**
The swimmer would start each 50 easy and build up the speed within the 50, finishing each 50 fast.

▶ **Negative Split Set**
The swimmer would negative split each 50 by swimming the second half of the 50 faster than the first half.

▶ **Warm Down**
The warm down is an easy swim like the warm up.

▶ **Feel for the Water**
Occurs when a swimmer can feel the effect each sculling motion has on the water, and can, at will, change the effort and speed at each section of the scull.

▶ **Taper**
The time of the season when a swimmer will gradually cut back on the amount of yardage performed in a workout.

▶ **Yardage**
The distance covered in an entire training session.

mentally. In a sport that is constantly telling you to work, work, work, it is the taper that is the key to success. And during the taper, you are doing everything *but* work. You are resting, concentrating on details, swimming easy, and kicking easy. The opposite of what you have been told the first two-thirds of the season.

When planning a training season it is important to not over set your goals and train too hard or too fast. This will only cause shoulder problems. In order to give training an honest effort you will have to create a schedule that will allow for 3 to 6 months of consistent training 2 to 3 times a week. Consistency and persistence will play an important role in your ability to master the sport of swimming.

SUMMARY

- In this chapter the swimmer learns how to train as a swimmer.
- The chapter starts with the importance of circle swimming and warming up before each training session.
- The discussion on training techniques such as interval training, build sets, and descend sets are all important to a daily workout schedule.

Appendix A

INTRODUCTORY TRAINING
LEVEL 1

▶ **Workout #1**

100 easy
200 swim
4 x 25 kick on your back
2 x 25 count your strokes (choice of strokes)
100 easy

25 = 1 length
*take 1–2 min. between sets

▶ **Workout #2**

100 easy
4 x 25 as slow as you can go
2 x 50 kick 1 minute rest in between
2 x 25 freestyle count your strokes
2 x 25 freestyle take one less stroke per 25
100 easy warm down

LEVEL 2

▶ **Workout #1**

300 easy choice, no butterfly
200 kick easy
2 x 150 swim :30 sec. rest
3 x 100 swim :20 sec. rest
3 x 50 swim :05 sec. rest
100 easy
25 = 1 length
*take 1–2 min. between sets

▶ **Workout #2**

300 easy warm up, no butterfly
4 x 50 kick :30 seconds rest
4 x 25 kick : 30 rest—build each 25
2 x 200 swim choice 1 min. rest
4 x 25 swim choice descend 1–4
100 easy warm down

LEVEL 3

▶ **Workout #1**

500 easy choice, no butterfly
3 x 200 swim :30
3 x 100 kick :15
10 x 25 count your strokes. Your choice of stroke. If you
    choose butterfly, do every other one fly.
4 x 25 take 2 less strokes than you did on the previous set.

100 easy

25 = 1 length

*take 1–2 min. between sets

▶ **Workout #2**

500 easy warm up, no butterfly

4 x 100 kick :15 seconds rest, no board

25, 50, 100 swim choice :15 second rest (swim a 25, :15 second rest, swim a 50, :15 sec. rest, and so on up and down the lane.)

100, 50, 25

4 x 25 stroke drills, your choice

100 easy warm down

Appendix

LEVEL 1

▶ **Group Workout**

warm up 500 slow as you can go

6 x 25 3-2-1 drill

3 x 25 head position goggles at waterline

2 x 25 chin on waterline

1 x 25 arm pit drill

2 x 25 skull drill 1/3, 1/3, 1/3

1 x 25 slow as you can go

300 perfect or 200 perfect

100 warm down

LEVEL 2

▶ **Group Workout**

warm up 600 as slow as you can go

300 kick, no board

10 x 25 swim descend 1–10

6 x 25 3-2-1 drill

2 x 25 goggles on the waterline

1 x 25 chin on the waterline

1 x 25 distance per stroke

1 x 25 with the number of strokes given
10 x 50 with the number of strokes given
200 easy

LEVEL 3

▶ **Workout**

warm up 500 as slow as you can go
10 x 25 free 1:00
200 kick
5 x 50 kick 2:00, 1:30, 1:15
10 x 50 build 1:30
10 x 25 1:30

LEVEL 4

▶ **Workout**

warm up 600 slow as you can go
10 x 50 free 1:00
300 kick easy
10 x 50 free kick
easy 50
10 x 50 build
300 easy

A Closer Look—Typical Week of Training for Tom Jager

Day 1
AM
6 x 500 k 2 without board
PM
1000 swim warm up
10 x 100 kick descend 1–10
10 x 100 swim descend 1–10
5 x 100 swim easy
5 x 100 kick easy
10 x 50 kick fly
10 x 50 swim odd fly even free
Day 2
PM
5 x 200 swim warm up #3,4 IM
10 x 50 kick 3, 5, 7, 10 last 10 blast
5 x 300 swim dps* blast the last one
5 x 300 kick blow
10 x 50 swim dps*
*Distance per stroke. Trying to take as
few of strokes per lap as possible but
still make moderate interval.
Day 3
AM
5 x 600 k 2 w/o board
pm
2 x 1000 swim easy
1 x 1000 kick easy
1 x 800 swim easy
1 x 1000 kick easy
200 swim easy

Day 4
AM
500 easy
4 x 300 swim
4 x 300 kick
10 x 50 kick fast 8–10
6 x 50 kick 6 strokes per 50
6 x 50 s dps
Day 5
AM
2 x 1500 k 1 w/o board
PM
500 s easy
20 x 100 k 3, 5, 7, 10 blast last 15 yards
20 x 100 s 3, 5, 7, 10 blast last 15 yards
2 x 250 swim dps distance per stroke
Day 6
AM
3 x 1000 k 1w/o board
Day 7
OFF

ADVANCED TRAINING

1) 500 swim easy
   20 x 100 kick 3,5,7,10 blast last 15
   20 x 100 swim 3,5,7,10 blast last 15
   2 x 250 working on distance over stroke
2) 500 swim easy
   100, 200, 300, 400, 400, 300, 200,100 kick easy/hard up/down
   100, 200, 300, 400, 400, 300, 200,100 swim easy/hard up/down
   10 x 50 (9 strokes per 25 yards)
3) 500 swim easy
   10 x 100 swim descend 1–10
   10 x 100 kick descend 1–10
   30 x 50 swim 50/50 fly/free
   20 x 50 kick 5, 10, 15, 20 underwater dolphin kick
4) 500 swim easy
   500 kick easy
   5 x 300 swim
   5 x 300 kick
   10 x 100 blast turns
5) 3000 choice
6) 500 swim easy
   500 kick easy
   10 x 50 swim blast first ten yards
   10 x 50 swim blast last ten yards
   10 x 100 kick time #10
   10 x 100 swim #5, 7, 50 fly 50 free
7) 500 easy swim
   kick 400, 300, 200, 100
   swim 100, 200, 300, 400
   200 easy
   20 x 50 5, 10, 15, 20 underwater no board
   200 easy warm down

SUGGESTED READING

The American Red Cross, 1992. *Swimming and Diving*. St. Louis: Mosby Lifeline.

Colwin, Cecil M. 1992. *Swimming into the 21st Century*. Champaign, IL: Human Kinetics Publishers.

Costill, D. L., E. W. Maglischo and A. B. Richardson. 1992. *Swimming*. Oxford: Blackwell Scientific Publications.

Rouse, Jeff. 1997. *The Young Swimmer: A Young Enthusiast's Guide To Swimming*. New York: DK Publishing, Inc.

Whitten, Phillip. 1994. *The Complete Book of Swimming*. New York: Random House, Inc.

INDEX

A

Advanced scull, 20
Alcohol, 6
Ankle stretch, 58
Arm pull, in freestyle, 25–26

B

Back stretches, 55–56, 59–60
Backstroke
  drills for, 38
  early recognition of, 2
  elementary, 20–21
  finishing in, 39–40
  mechanics of, 34–38
  starts for, 38–39
  turns for, 39
Backstroke flags, 12, 39
Beginners' exercises, 17–22. *See also*
  Appendix A
Body position
  for backstroke, 35
  for breaststroke, 42
  for butterfly, 49, 50
Breaststroke
  early recognition of, 2
  finishing in, 46
  mechanics of, 42–44
  performance tips for, 44, 46
  starts for, 45
  turns for, 45, 46
Breaststroke kick, 19, 43–44
Breathing
  in backstroke, 37–38
  in breaststroke, 42
  in butterfly, 51–52
  controlled, 8
  in freestyle, 29–30
  learning, 18, 19
Bubble blowing, 18
Build set, 64, 65
Butterfly
  advent of, 2
  finishing in, 53
  mechanics of, 48–52

Butterfly—*Cont.*
  performance tips for, 48
  starts for, 52
  turns for, 52–53

C

Caps, 14, 15
Cardiovascular benefits, 7
Chlorine damage, 13–14
Circle swimming, 62, 63
Competition
  Easter Island race, 2
  facilities and equipment for, 12–14
  opportunities for, 8
  training for, 64–66 *(see also Appendix A)*
Conditioning
  monitoring, 7
  stretching for, 54–60
  workout schedules, 61–66 *(see also*
    Appendix A)
  See also Fitness swimming
Controlled breathing, 8

D

Deck, safety on, 6
Descending set, 63–64
Diving safety, 5–6
Dolphin kick, 51, 52
Drag finger tips drill, 30
Drugs, 6
Dry land exercises, 62, 63. *See also* Stretching

E

Easter Island race, 2
Elementary backstroke, 20–21
Equipment, 12–16
Exercise, swimming as. *See* Fitness
  swimming
Exercises
  kicking, 18–19
  scheduling, 61–66
  sculling, 19–20
  stretching, 54–60
  See also Stroke drills
Exhaling, 18

77